ROBERTS' RULES
OF
LESBIAN BREAK-UPS

Shelly Roberts

Spinsters Ink
Duluth, Minnesota

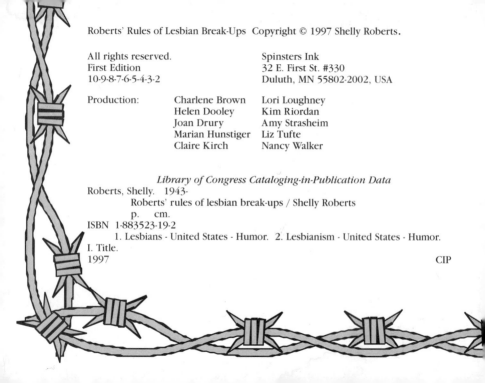

Roberts' Rules of Lesbian Break-Ups Copyright © 1997 Shelly Roberts.

All rights reserved.
First Edition
10-9-8-7-6-5-4-3-2

Spinsters Ink
32 E. First St. #330
Duluth, MN 55802-2002, USA

Production: Charlene Brown   Lori Loughney
               Helen Dooley   Kim Riordan
               Joan Drury   Amy Strasheim
               Marian Hunstiger Liz Tufte
               Claire Kirch   Nancy Walker

Library of Congress Cataloging-in-Publication Data
Roberts, Shelly. 1943-
     Roberts' rules of lesbian break-ups / Shelly Roberts
        p.   cm.
ISBN 1-883523-19-2
     1. Lesbians - United States - Humor. 2. Lesbianism - United States - Humor.
I. Title.
1997   CIP

Dedication

I've been in a monogamous relationship for the past twenty-four years . . . and they were six of the nicest people you'd ever want to meet.

To B & S & B & R & J1 & J1 & J1 & J1 & J1 & J1 & J2 for sharing the experience.

And to all the wonderful lesbian women of the Internet on-line community who were willing to share their own experiences, who, blessedly, kept this from becoming an autobiography.

—Shelly

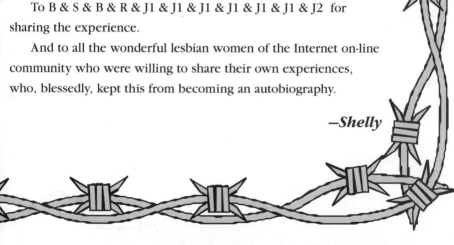

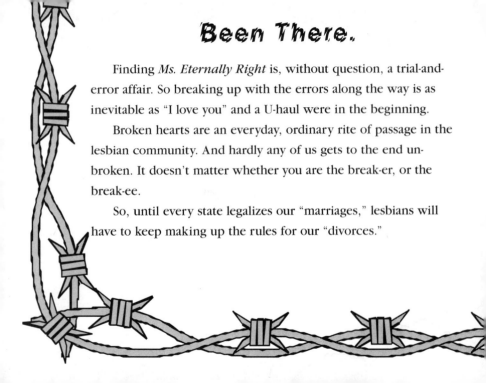

Been There.

Finding *Ms. Eternally Right* is, without question, a trial-and-error affair. So breaking up with the errors along the way is as inevitable as "I love you" and a U-haul were in the beginning.

Broken hearts are an everyday, ordinary rite of passage in the lesbian community. And hardly any of us gets to the end unbroken. It doesn't matter whether you are the break-er, or the break-ee.

So, until every state legalizes our "marriages," lesbians will have to keep making up the rules for our "divorces."

Done That.

In spite of all the Lesbian High Drama, however, it is just barely possible that there is something funny in all this.

Which is good, because it has now been scientifically confirmed (in a study on gay male twins, of course), contrary to popular opinion, it only *heals* when you laugh.

Next time, maybe it will be a little easier if you have at least *some* idea of the rules.

Your mileage, as always, may vary.

—Shelly

They *were* right.
She *wasn't*
good enough for you.

There is *still* no such thing
as lesbian divorce.
There is only
thermonuclear war.

2

And then best friends.

3

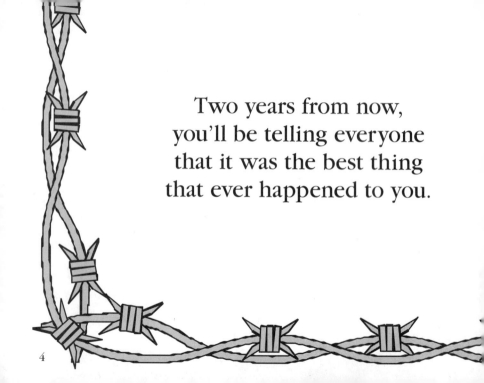

Two years from now,
you'll be telling everyone
that it was the best thing
that ever happened to you.

4

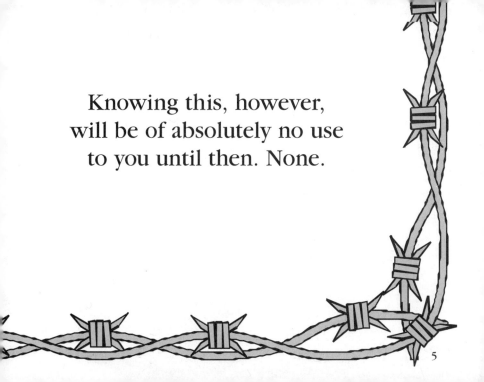

Knowing this, however,
will be of absolutely no use
to you until then. None.

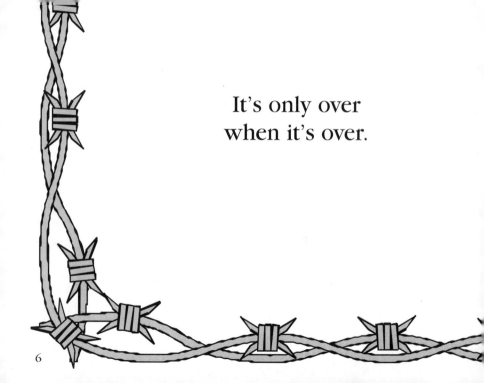

It's only over
when it's over.

6

But
not *necessarily.*

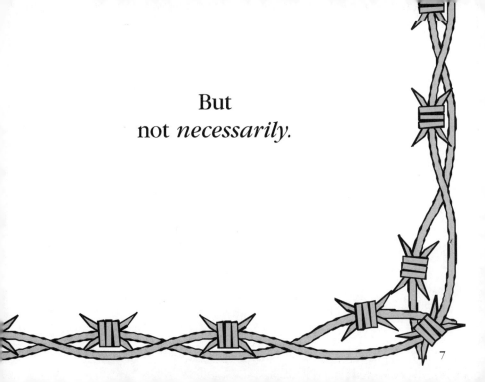

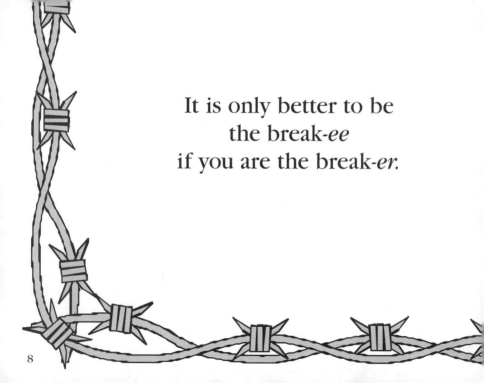

It is only better to be
the break-*ee*
if you are the break-*er*.

8

And vice versa.

She may not be doing it
to you.

She may just be *doing* it.

You will not like her
new girlfriend.

12

Unless *you* chose her.

In which case,
she may not like
her new girlfriend.

This will change
in a number of years.

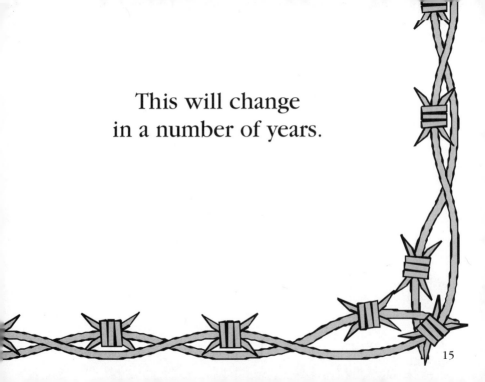

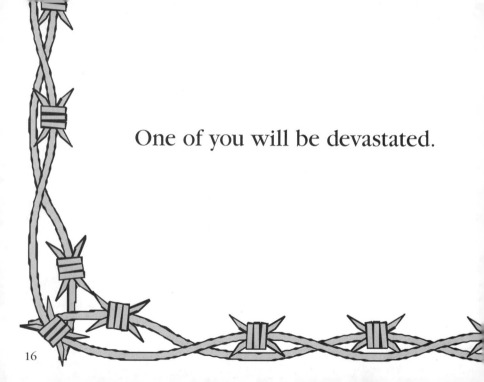

One of you will be devastated.

Everyone will be
surprised by which one.
(Including *you*.)

She is not the woman
you first married.

18

Perhaps she never was.

19

It *is* possible to have a
good break-up.

Not *common.*
Not *ordinary.*
Not *usual.*
But possible.

21

No matter what she says,
she doesn't *really*
want to hear about
your new lover.

22

Especially not
in excruciating detail.

23

Ditto how much better the sex is.

Pain hurts.

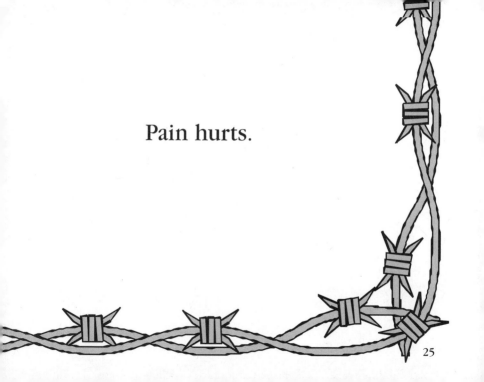

Get your own lawyer.

Take a year off.

There is great satisfaction
in giving her piano
to the Salvation Army.

Or rolling it
down the stairs.

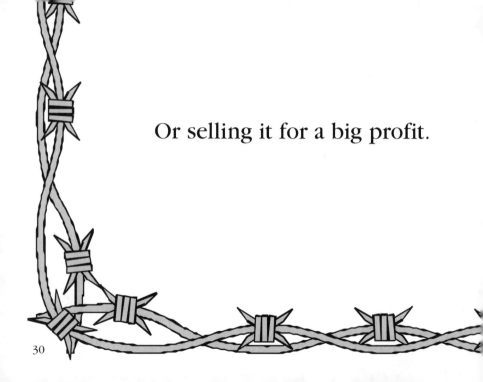

Or selling it for a big profit.

Or filling it with Cool Whip
and black cherry Jello
just before her
moving people get there.

She *used to be*
your best friend.
She may well
someday in the future
be your best friend again.

But during a break-up,
you need a *new* best friend.

REVENGE
is completely and totally
ignoring her.

The stereo system
is the hardest thing
to divide.

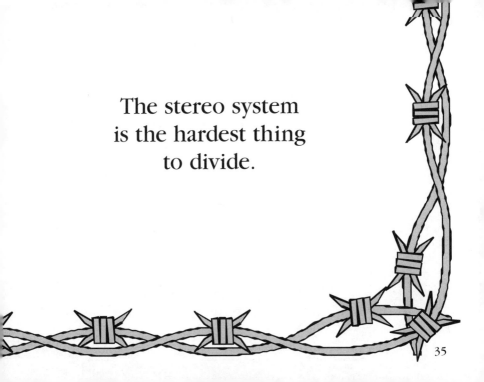

Not having sex
with anyone but yourself
is much more a symptom
of being *long* married
than of being *not* married.

There is no such thing as
happily-ever-after.
Sigh.

If you stand in front of
a full-length mirror
and see a raving beauty . . .

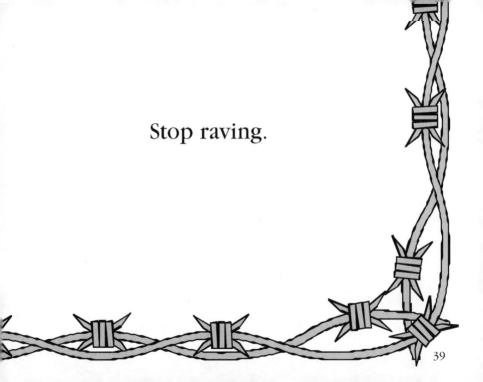

Stop raving.

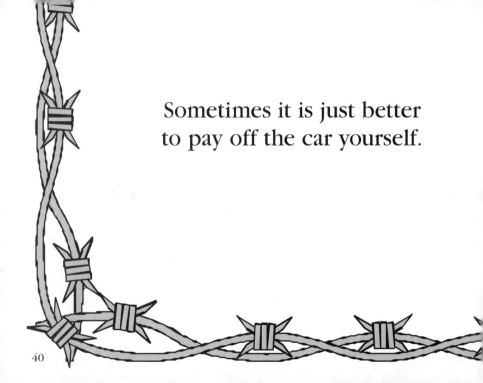

Sometimes it is just better
to pay off the car yourself.

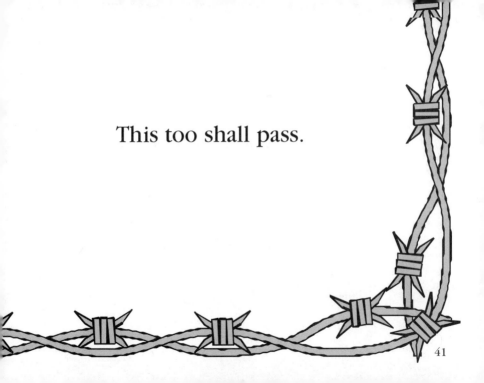

This too shall pass.

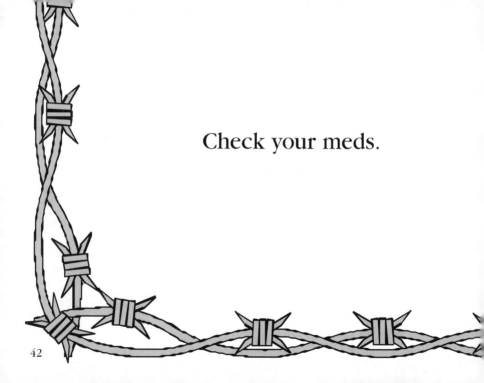

Check your meds.

Ancient Lesbianese Saying:

In a court of law,
she who has the most signatures
on the cancelled checks
wins.

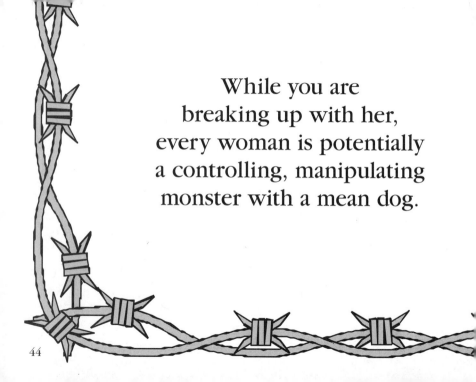

While you are
breaking up with her,
every woman is potentially
a controlling, manipulating
monster with a mean dog.

44

Even the good ones.

Nearly everyone
sleeps with her Ex
at least *once*
without getting arrested.

The *real* winner
is the long-distance carrier
of your choice.

Get *her* to move.

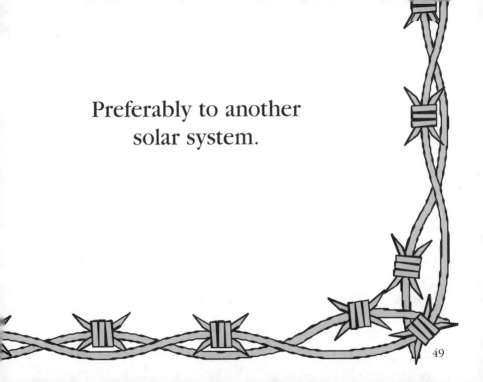

Preferably to another
solar system.

49

Kindness counts.

Someone *is* keeping score.

51

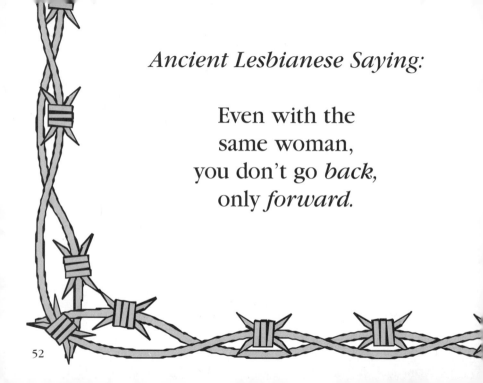

Ancient Lesbianese Saying:

Even with the
same woman,
you don't go *back*,
only *forward*.

It has been
scientifically established
that there are precisely
– 0 –
good ways
to break the news.

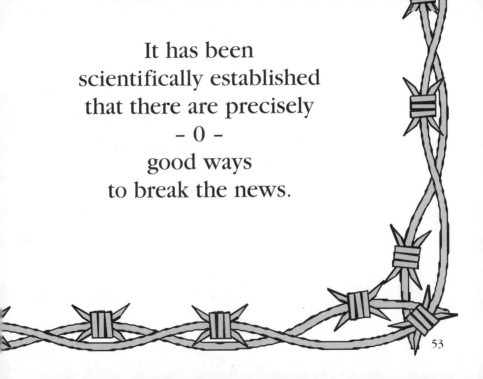

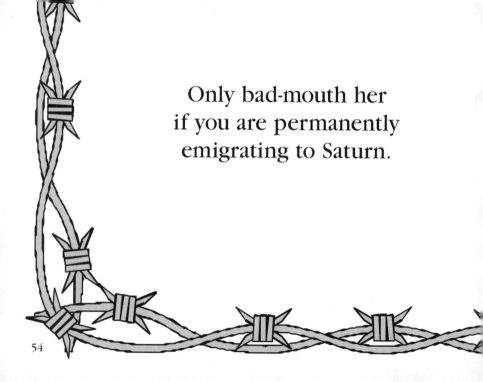

Only bad-mouth her
if you are permanently
emigrating to Saturn.

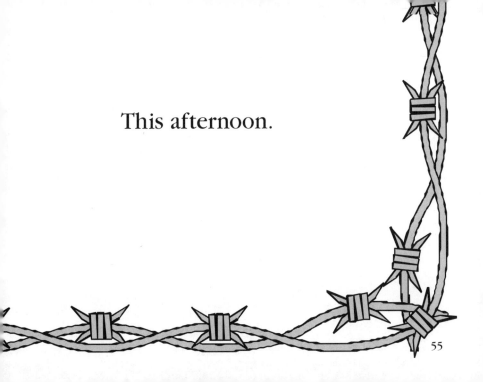

This afternoon.

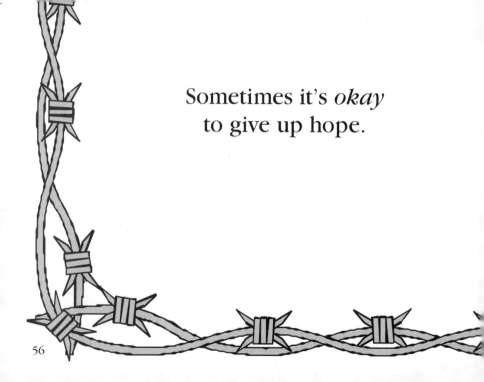

Sometimes it's *okay*
to give up hope.

It depends on what
you were hoping for.

She *will* lie about
what really happened.

But, hey, so will *you*.

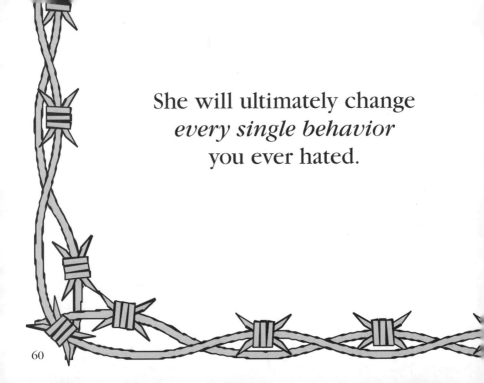

She will ultimately change
every single behavior
you ever hated.

Unfortunately,
she won't do it until
after you're long gone.

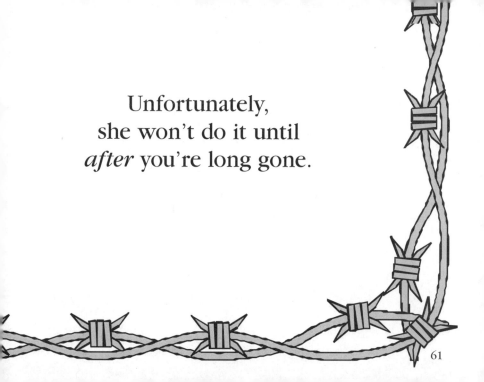

Your friends will agree
that she was awful.

Her friends will all
believe *her.*

This *is*
what friends are for.

If you two
get back together,
it's illegal
to hold it against them.

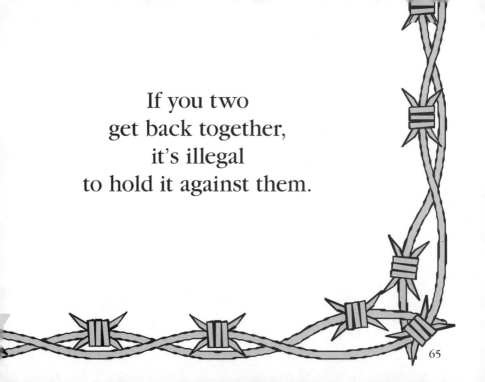

The single biggest
cause of break-ups
is:

WALLPAPERING!

Never promise in writing
to support her for the
rest of her life
unless you are using
disappearing ink.

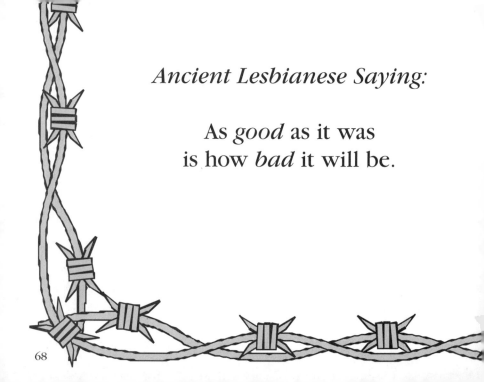

Ancient Lesbianese Saying:

As *good* as it was
is how *bad* it will be.

Ancient Lesbianese Saying:

As *bad* as it was
is how *good* it will be.

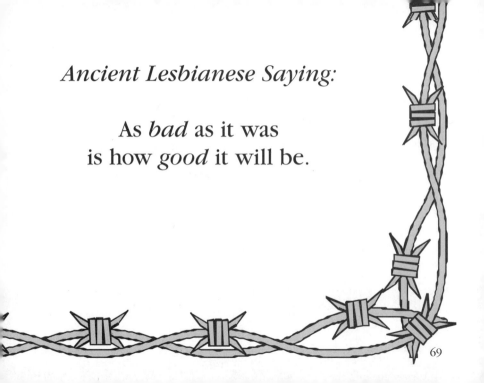

No matter what
your shrink says,
no couples ever survive
couples' counseling
. . . for long.

The Ex of your Ex
is fair game.

If you remembered her birthday
three weeks late,
you're done.

NEXT TIME:
Buy *two* copies
of autographed books.

73

Crazy-*in*-love is kindergarten
compared to
crazy *out* of it.

There is *always* a hidden agenda.

You don't mourn
the relationship you *had*.

You mourn the relationship
you *hoped* you'd have.

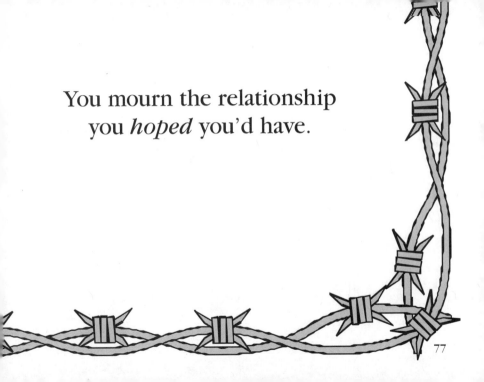

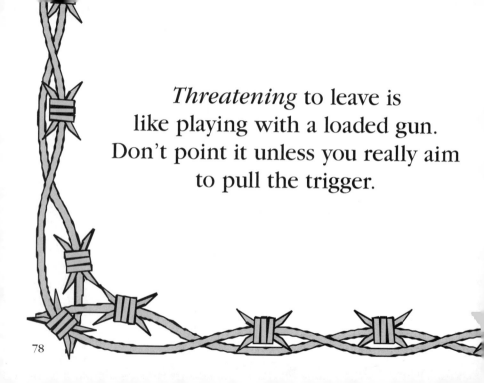

Threatening to leave is
like playing with a loaded gun.
Don't point it unless you really aim
to pull the trigger.

Remember the kid
who cried
WOLF!

Your friends will *try*
not to take sides.

Ancient Lesbianese Saying:

Do not lend your Ex
your car, your girlfriend,
or your credit card
for at least six months.

When you gotta go,
you–*sigh*–well, you know.

Just say "Good-bye."

83

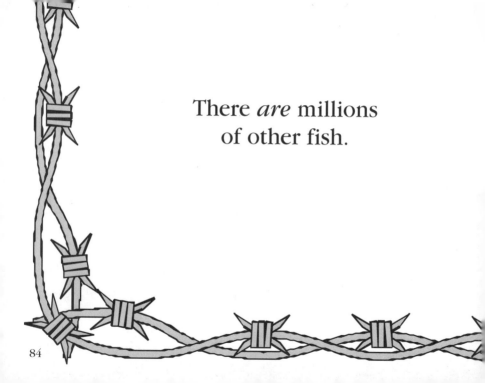

There *are* millions
of other fish.

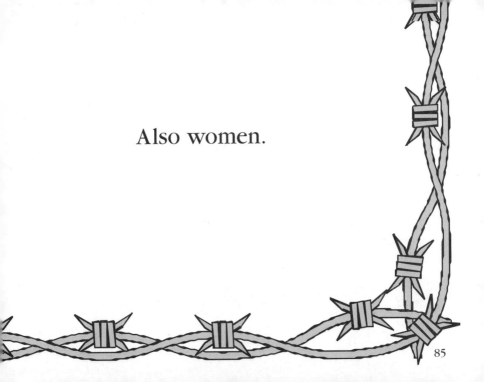

Also women.

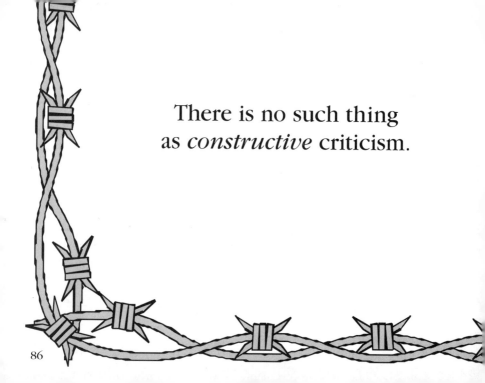

There is no such thing
as *constructive* criticism.

REVENGE
is winning the lottery
NOW!

Drinking is
short-term thinking.

Everyone
has problems with intimacy.

Breaking up takes practice.

"Nobody's perfect"
is a truism, not an alibi.

Don't gloat.

"Support" and "control"
are not synonyms.

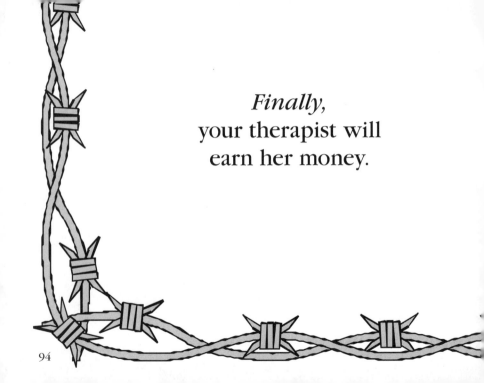

Finally,
your therapist will
earn her money.

Get a friend to watch over
her move out.
It's *not*
a do-it-yourself project.

The last piece of pie
is *yours*.

Chocolate can only help.

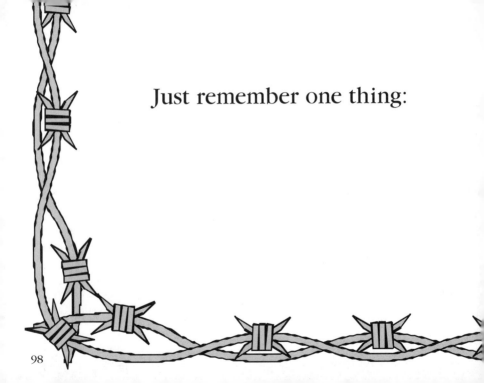

Just remember one thing:

One day at a time.
One inch at a time.
One problem at a time.
One step at a time.
One foot in front of the other.

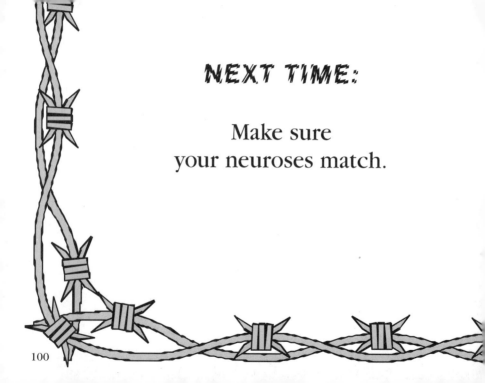

NEXT TIME:

Make sure
your neuroses match.

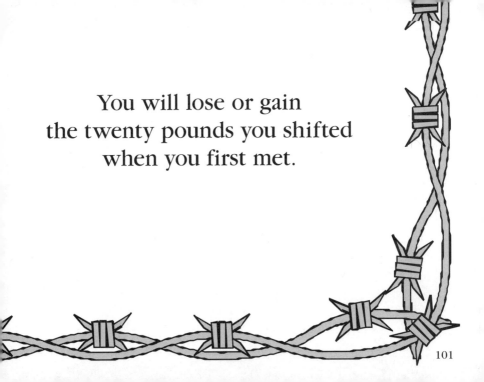

You will lose or gain
the twenty pounds you shifted
when you first met.

Throwing furniture
at someone
is not considered kosher
and will be counted
against you.

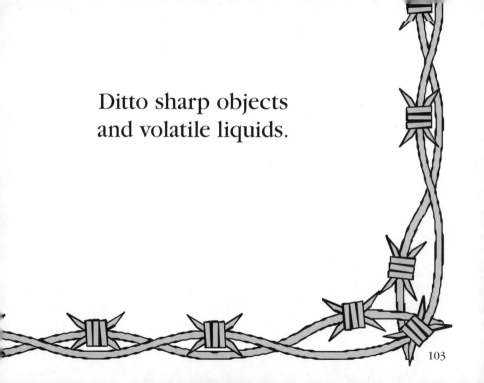

Ditto sharp objects
and volatile liquids.

You will follow strangers
wearing *her* perfume.

After a while,
you will stop.
Or get arrested by mall security.

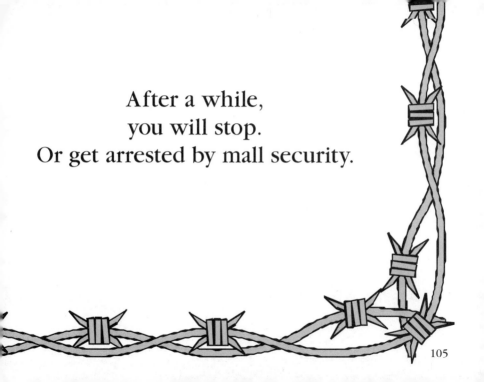

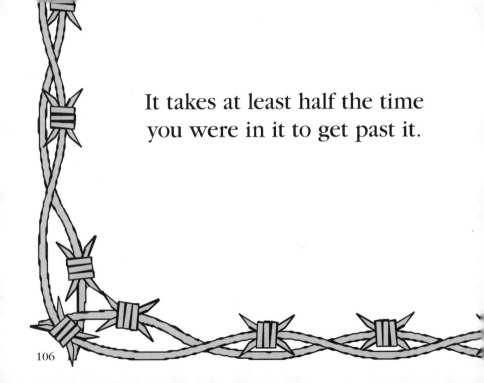

It takes at least half the time
you were in it to get past it.

No matter which side
you are on.

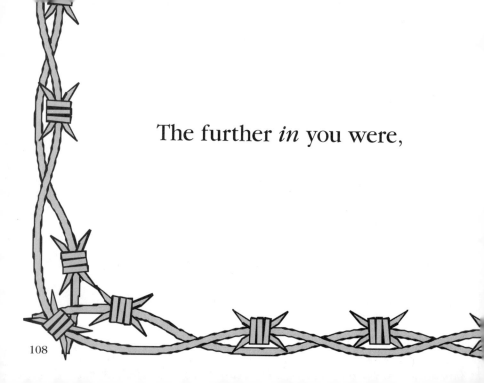

The further *in* you were,

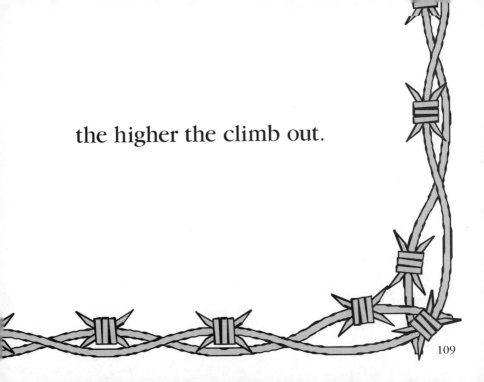

the higher the climb out.

Leave *clean.*

And leave *quick.*

Keep the cat.

If you can't pay
your friends back
with time and attention,
try offering housework
or sending flowers.

The break-*ee*
gets the most stuff.

Unless the break-*er*
owns the house.

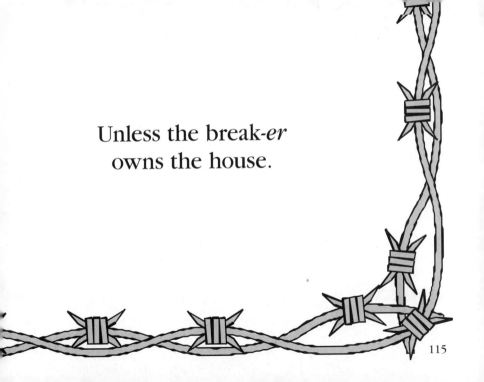

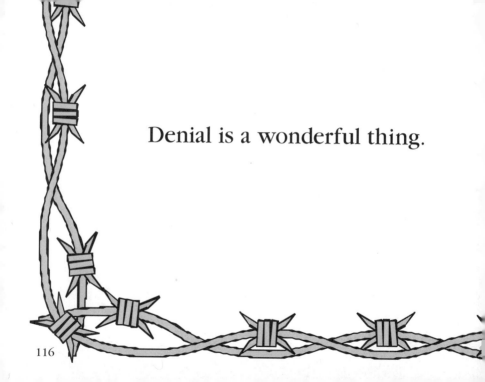

Denial is a wonderful thing.

REVENGE
is having her dog
follow *you* home.

117

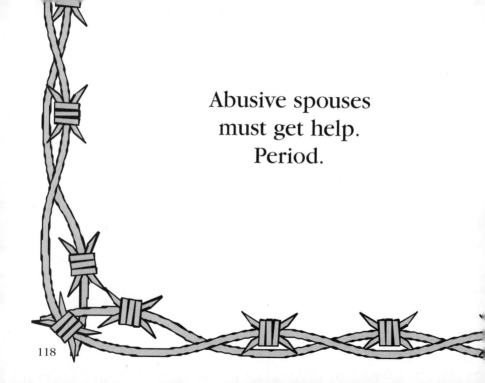

Abusive spouses
must get help.
Period.

Abused spouses
must get help.
Period.

Demand alone time.
Then remember to take it.

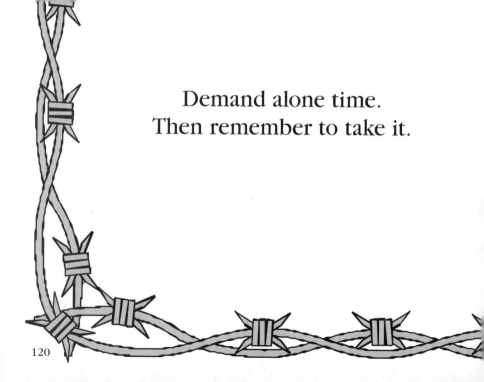

Let go when it's time.
*(Or, for the sake of your friends
and your Exes,
at least within the first
six to seven years.)*

121

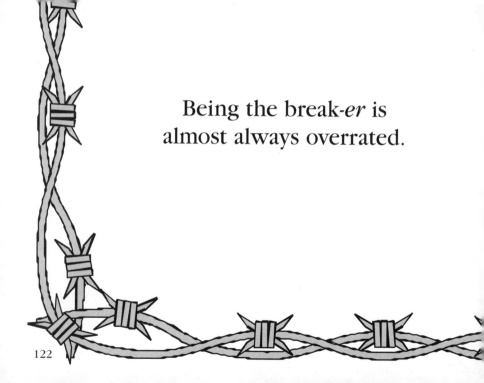

Being the break-*er* is
almost always overrated.

You *did* deserve better treatment.

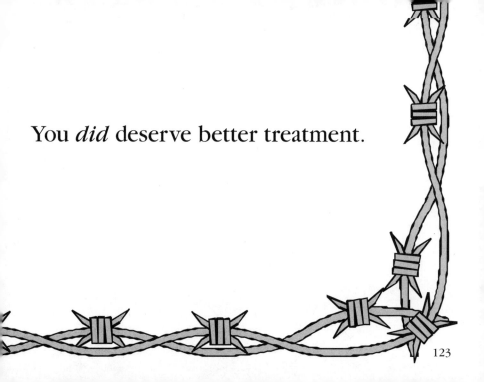

Writing it all down
does help.

124

Finding your next lover
helps more.

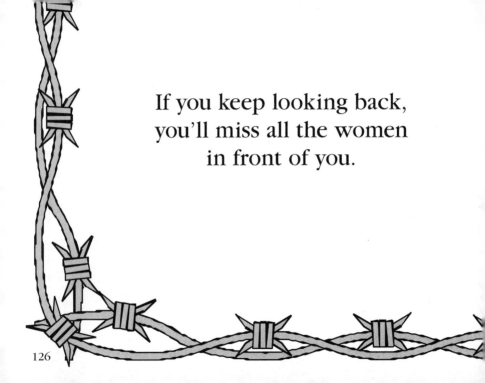

If you keep looking back,
you'll miss all the women
in front of you.

Volunteer for everything
(except masochism).

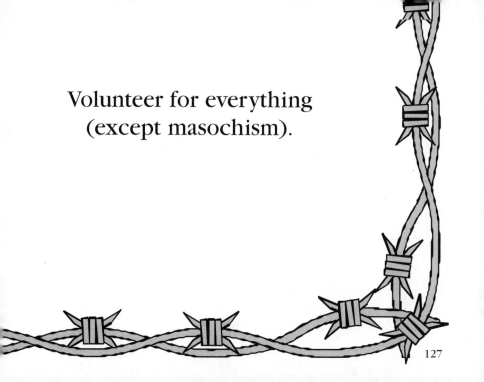

Sending death threats
is a felony.

They won't make
an exception in *your* case
just because she
really, really, really
deserves them.

If you want her
in your life *later* . . .

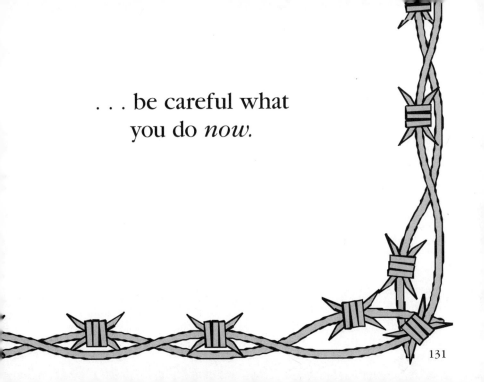

. . . be careful what you do *now*.

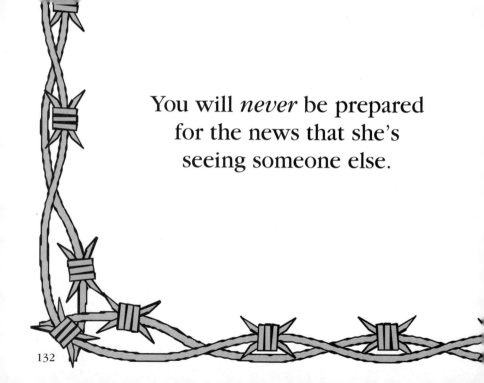

You will *never* be prepared
for the news that she's
seeing someone else.

Never send flowers
if you are the break-*ee*.

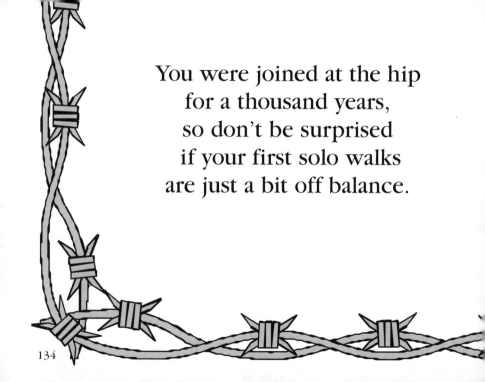

You were joined at the hip
for a thousand years,
so don't be surprised
if your first solo walks
are just a bit off balance.

If you keep the cats,
get kitty support.

LESBIAN CONUNDRUM
PART 1:

It is difficult to live together
as though you were going
to break up.

LESBIAN CONUNDRUM
PART 2:

It is difficult to break up
if you lived as though
you wouldn't.

The longer you stay single,
the better you get at it.

What you can't do for yourself,
you can *hire*.

Falling *in* love,
all the music suddenly makes sense.

Falling *out* of it,
all the self-help books do.

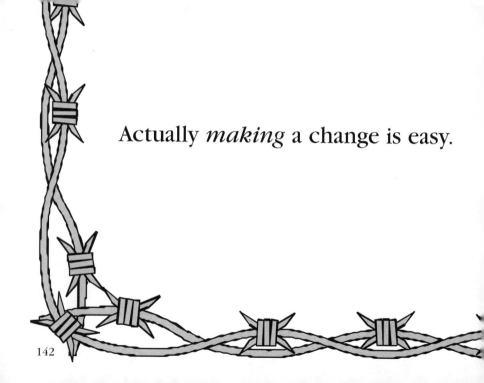

Actually *making* a change is easy.

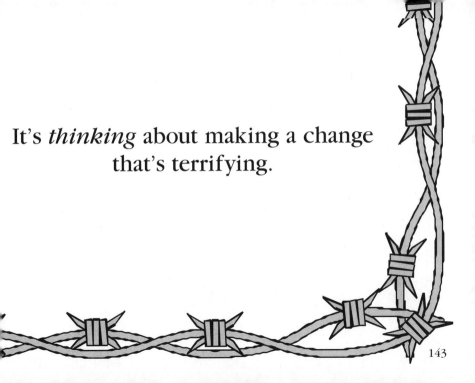

It's *thinking* about making a change that's terrifying.

Once you don't care anymore,
she isn't nearly as bad
as you thought.

144

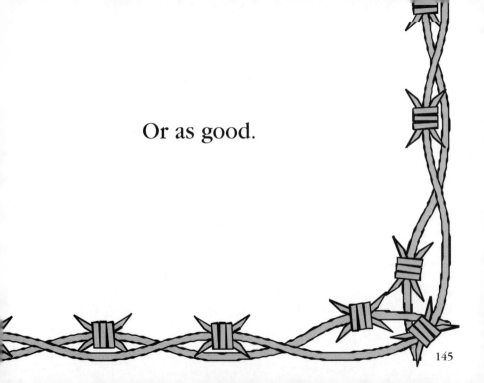

Or as good.

Just because you can't
get married,

doesn't mean you *weren't* married.

She *did* tell you
exactly who she was.
In the first three weeks.

You just weren't
listening carefully.

Any relationship
that makes you wonder if
you have a personality disorder
is pretty much done.

Don't ask mutual friends
to keep secrets.

Separate out of love,
not anger.

Trying to
soften the impact
hardens the blow.

Your relationship didn't fail.
It just ran out of time.

Opposites may *attract,*
but they rarely last.

REVENGE
is taking out the
restraining order *first*.

It's bad form to bring
your *new* girlfriend
to get your *old* things.

157

There *is* sanity.
It's at the *other* end
of your rope.

It was an addiction.
It was an addiction.
It was an addiction.

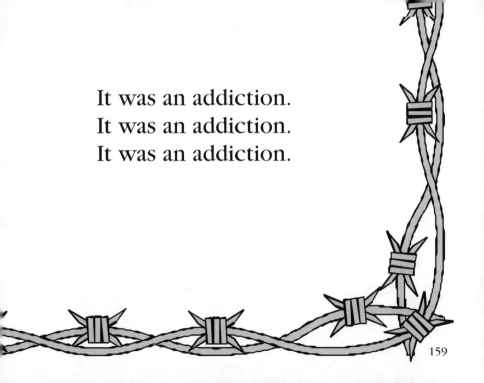

Make friends with
plug-in appliances.

Denial *is* a wonderful thing.

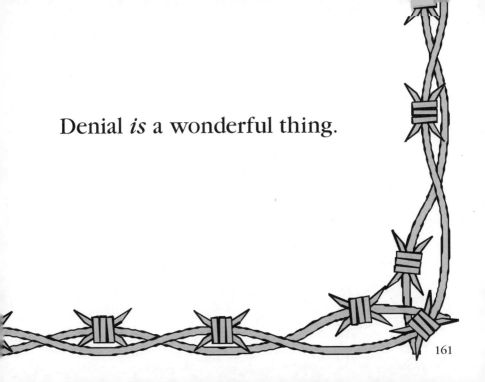

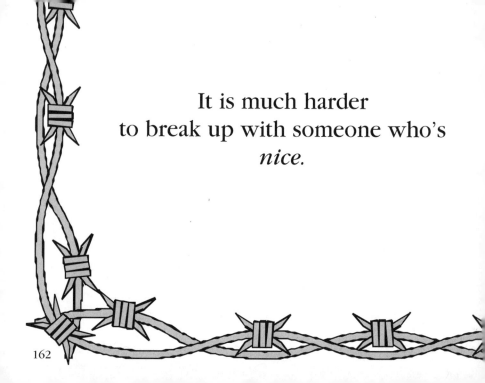

It is much harder
to break up with someone who's
nice.

Or someone you like.

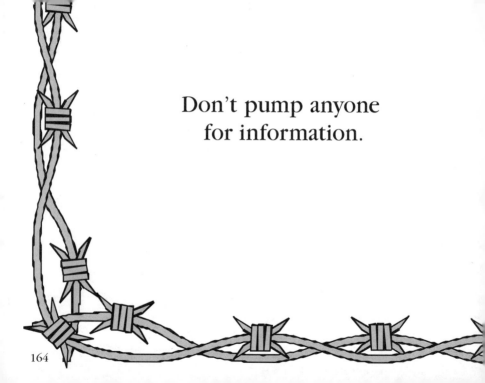

Don't pump anyone
for information.

Unless you really want
to know it.

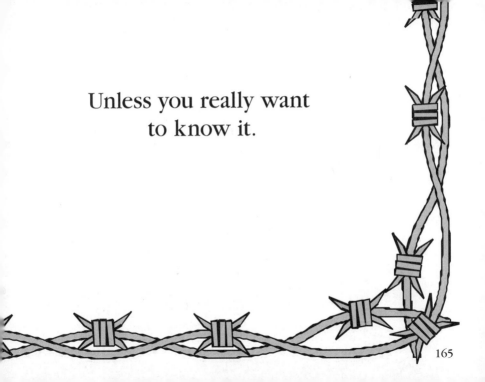

If she was your therapist,
report her.

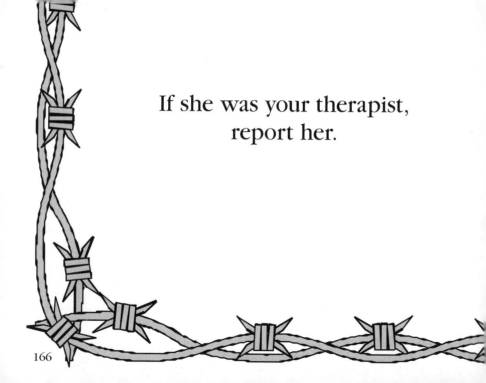

The secret formula
for survival
is made up of equal parts
Häagen Dazs, Godiva, and Prozac.

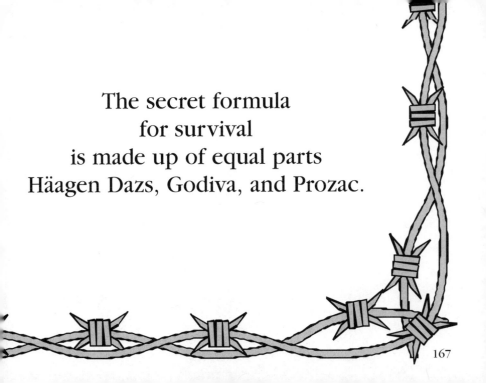

You can't explain
where she is to the dog.
Fido is a dumb animal.

Try to remember
that you aren't.

You can't fix her
if she doesn't know she's broken.

In fact, you can't fix her
at all.

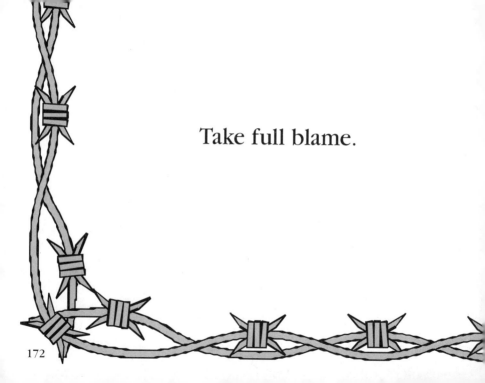

Take full blame.

Your friends will respect you for it,
and it'll drive *her* nuts.

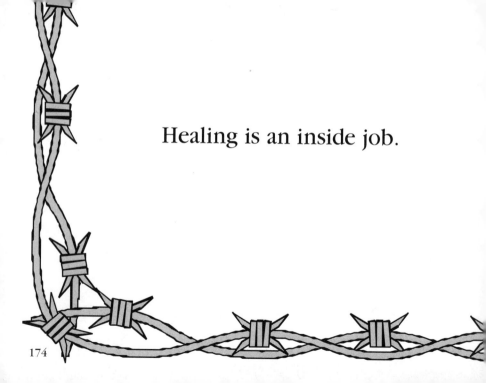

Healing is an inside job.

174

NEXT TIME:
Date nicer women.

Spinsters Ink was founded in 1978 to produce vital books for diverse women's communities. In 1986 we merged with Aunt Lute Books to become Spinsters/Aunt Lute. In 1990, the Aunt Lute Foundation became an independent, nonprofit publishing program. In 1992, Spinsters moved to Minnesota.

Spinsters Ink is committed to publishing novels and nonfiction works by women that deal with significant issues from a feminist perspective: books that not only name crucial issues in women's lives, but more importantly, encourage change and growth; books that help make the best in our lives more possible.

Other Titles Available From Spinsters Ink

The Activist's Daughter, Ellyn Bache	$10.95
All the Muscle You Need, Diana McRae	$8.95
Amazon Story Bones, Ellen Frye	$10.95
As You Desire, Madeline Moore	$9.95
Being Someone, Ann MacLeod	$9.95
Cancer in Two Voices, 2nd Ed., Butler & Rosenblum	$12.95
Child of Her People, Anne Cameron	$10.95
Common Murder, Val McDermid	$9.95
Considering Parenthood, Cheri Pies	$12.95
Deadline for Murder, Val McDermid	$10.95
Desert Years, Cynthia Rich	$7.95
Elise, Claire Kensington	$7.95
Fat Girl Dances with Rocks, Susan Stinson	$10.95
Final Rest, Mary Morell	$9.95
Final Session, Mary Morell	$9.95

Other Titles Available From Spinsters Ink

A Gift of the Emperor, Therese Park	$10.95
Give Me Your Good Ear, 2nd Ed., Maureen Brady	$9.95
Goodness, Martha Roth	$10.95
The Hangdog Hustle, Elizabeth Pincus	$9.95
High and Outside, Linnea A. Due	$8.95
The Journey, Anne Cameron	$9.95
Lesbian Erotic Dance, JoAnn Loulan	$12.95
Lesbian Passion, JoAnn Loulan	$12.95
Lesbian Sex, JoAnn Loulan	$12.95
Lesbians at Midlife, Sang, Warshow, & Smith	$12.95
The Lessons, Melanie McAllester	$9.95
Life Savings, Linnea Due	$10.95
Living at Night, Mariana Romo-Carmona	$10.95
Look Me in the Eye, 2nd Ed., Macdonald & Rich	$8.95
Love and Memory, Amy Oleson	$9.95

Other Titles Available From Spinsters Ink

Spinsters Ink titles are available at your local booksellers or by mail order through Spinsters Ink. A free catalog is available upon request. Please include $2.00 for the first title ordered and 50¢ for every title thereafter. Visa and Mastercard accepted. Please contact us for author appearances and signings.

Spinsters Ink

32 E. First St., #330

Duluth, MN 55802-2002

USA

218-727-3222 (Phone) (Fax) 218-727-3119

(E-mail) spinsters@aol.com

(Internet) http://www.lesbian.org/spinsters-ink

The #1 best-selling author of ***Roberts Rules of Lesbian Living,*** Shelly divides time working for interesting communications clients, finding the common threads and surrealism in everyday lesbian life, working on happily-ever-after, and cyber-hangin' with the lesbianetters. Sleeping, not on her current agenda, may soon become a viable option.

As usual, nobody knows what rules she'll proclaim next. Stay tuned.

Having ridden the hook-and-ladder truck in the '96 Atlanta Pride Parade, and jump-seated in the cockpit of a Boeing 727 researching a video for an air-cargo company, **Shelly Roberts** has been lately pondering gender definitions and psychosexual role modeling. As a result, she's stopped proclaiming that there's a secret seven-year-old boy in her, trying to get out. She's now convinced that it was a seven-year-old *girl* whom nobody bothered to tell that liking fire trucks and jet airplanes was perfectly fine.

Shelly now figures, hey, what's the worst they could do? Call her a *lesbian? (Nyah, Nyah, Nyah-Nyah, Nyah, Nyah. Too late!)*